TABLE OF CONTENTS

CHAPTER ONE
BUDGETING

Budgeting is never fun, especially when money is tight and it seems as though you can never get ahead financially. I will give you a few ideas on how to save some money, pay off debt, have some money in the bank, and not feel deprived. So, get out a piece of paper and lets get started.

I would like you to make a list of all of your debts. This is not easy, especially if you have a lot of debt, but an action plan will make you more motivated to get out of the hole.

Start by looking into the interest rate on each of your credit cards. The key here is to reduce your monthly payments by transferring them to a lower balance/lower interest rate card. If your cards are maxed out or almost maxed out, try to shop around for credit cards that have a high limit and that has a lower interest rate than what your paying now. Then transfer your balances onto that card. The money you save by not paying the higher interest rate can go directly to savings (if you have a high interest savings account) or add it to the principal of the credit card. This may seem small, but the credit card companies make big money on interest payments and late fees.

Even if you decide not to open a new card or transfer balances, I would like to recommend calling the credit card companies and see if they can reduce any of the interest rates just in case. Perhaps you have a good history with them, have been a customer a long time, and pay on time each month. It is possible they may give you a break.

Speaking of late fees, have you had any lately? Late fees are pricy and can suck up a big portion of your paycheck if you let it get out of hand. Many transactions are electronic these days, so sign up to have your bills automatically withdrawn from your account every month (auto pay). Not only will it save you overdraft fees, it will save you the time and effort of not having to make an online payment or write out a check, going to the post office, buying stamps, and waiting for the money to credit to the account. These few tips alone will save you a lot of money and time.

Shopping around for cheap health and auto insurance would also save you some money. Ask your friends and family who they use, what they pay, and how much it covers. It is also never too late to get life insurance as well if you have a family. Life insurance is relatively cheap these days and a good investment in case of death.

Now lets make two lists of priorities before we start with the actual budget. One list should be for saving money and the other should be paying off debt. In every budget, you should pay yourself first. This should go to savings. Part of your saving should go into retirement, part should go to an emergency fund, and the last part should go for a rainy day fund- this may include a vacation, getting some extra clothes, or just having some fun.

A key for success in paying off debt is to start with the debt that has the highest interest rate- whether it be a credit card, payday lending loan, or something else. If all of your debts have similar interest rates, and you don't owe any payday lenders, focus on the credit cards first. Pay the credit card that has the least amount owed on it. Move on to the next lowest one.

After that, move on to paying on the car note, then focus on the student loans and mortgage, putting part of the new freed up money your not paying to the credit card companies (or other companies) towards this. Some will called the snowball effect. If your underwater on your mortgage, it would make sense to really focus on paying extra on the mortgage.

Lets talk briefly about any money you may owe to friends or family. If you owe friends and family money, how important is it to you to pay them back? If that's pretty important to you, put it highest on your list of debt repayment priorities.

After you get all of your credit card debt and any unsecured debt taken care of, start putting the rest of that money your not going to put towards your mortgage into your retirement and other savings you may have for the future. Also, keep watching the money you spend. This is very important so you don't get caught up in the trap of debt.

Now that you have started on the above goals, lets get into the actual dollars and cents for every month. Write down your daily essential bills, like rent (or mortgage), food, insurance, electric, cable, phone, gym pass, or anything else that you pay money for.

Look at all your receipts for last month and write it all down. If you don't have any, then start tomorrow and gather all your receipts for one entire month. Include everything you use auto pay for as well. Writing it all down into categories on Excel is a great start.

Once you have everything written down, I'm sure you'll be surprised how much money you spend. Do you spend more money than you earn? If so, perhaps you can start earning a little extra money on the side doing something you already know how to do, like walking dogs, delivering pizzas, driving for Uber/Lyft,ect. This doesn't have to be long term, just until you can start saving a little more money.

When I started to do budgets, I didn't realize how much money I was actually spending on food and unnecessary things. You can easily save some money here without being deprived. Look through your coupon that you get in the mail. You can also use some online tools as well, like coupons.com. Start buying in bulk and get creative as well.

There are places you can go to pick fresh fruit for little cost- this can be a lot of fun if you bring your kids along and make a day of family time. Growing your own garden can save you some money as well, they just require a small investment and labor.

Saving money on food is easy, once you get the hang of it. It just comes down to your priorities and how much time your willing to put into it. Start making a game out of it with your spouse and kids. For example, you save X amount on food, then you can spend Y on something fun (just make sure Y is less than X here). Once you get the hang of it, saving money on food becomes a good habit you won't think much of.

Just make sure to make a separate listing for dining out. If you only want to spend $100 on eating out this month, put that $100 in an envelope and when its gone for the month, its gone.

If your spending more money on things that isn't necessarily important, it's time to fine tune your rainy day fund. After you've started putting money into your retirement fund and emergency fund, look at how much you have left over after all your necessary payments like rent and the water bill. (Don't forget to put an incidental list on things you need to pay every month, like shampoo and toilet paper).

How to Make a Budget

First, you need to know what to include in your budget. You should have sections for daily expenses, weekly expenses, monthly expenses, quarterly expenses, bi annual expenses, and annual expenses. You should also include sections for savings, entertainment, clothing, emergency savings, tithing (charity giving), Christmas savings, and anything else that you spend money on.

Second, you cannot figure in tax returns or any extras as income unless it is a specific amount that you can count on. You need to have your budget set up with your job income and only your job income. Treat these extras as extras and save some of them and use some to take your family out.

Third, if you are a married couple or a couple living together, then you cannot count the other person income at all. For example, what if she becomes pregnant and cannot work. You would have to completely readjust your budget. This is something you can easily avoid by just simply counting her income as savings and extra. Use it as spending money and as savings so that you will have a cushion when an emergency arises.

How to Make a Budget and Control Your Finances

Learning how to make a budget can be one of the most important financial decisions anyone ever makes. It can be the one thing that saves many people from financial ruin simply because it allows them to take back control of their money. The goal of any budget is to ensure that you and your family have the necessary money to cover life's necessities. Once those are covered any left over money can be used for any number of things, including fun and entertainment. The other thing to remember is that a monthly budget is like a living thing, with changing income, expenses and other things affecting it each month.

A budget is nothing more than some simple accounting that even kids can do. The ultimate goal of any budget is to have more money coming in than going out in bills each month. This may appear to be common sense, but unfortunately many people have a hard time making this happen, because they have no idea where their money is going. The paycheck gets deposited and before they know it all the money is gone until next pay day.

The best way to get started making a budget is to simply write down all your pertinent financial information on a piece of paper. There are free budget sheets that can be found on the internet that are useful in helping you get a good start on the budgeting process. You can also use a spreadsheet or budget software, but it is easiest to just start by writing it down with pencil and paper.

Determining your income is the first step in how to make your budget. If your job is your only source of income, look at your paycheck. Your income is the actual amount of the check, not the biggest number shown on the check. The biggest amount on the check is your gross income, which means no taxes have been deducted yet. Your net income, which you will use in making your budget, is the gross income minus all taxes and other payroll deductions. If you have other income sources such as a second job, child support, or alimony, these count as income too. Add all these income sources together.

The next step in how to make your budget is determining your expenses. This is harder than it sounds. The amount surprises many people. Make a list of every bill and expense you pay on a regular basis. These expenses include rent, mortgage, utilities, car insurance, home insurance, groceries, gasoline, parking fees, and even pet expenses. Use your checkbook register to help you remember the bills you pay. Some of these expenses change monthly, such as utility bills and credit card payments. Use an average or best guess for these. Add all these expenses together.

Once you have your income and expenses added up all you have to do is compare the two amounts. Your budget is balanced if the income column is greater than the expense column. If the expenses are greater than the income then you can use your written budget to start eliminating and cutting expenses to try and balance your income and outgoing cash flows.

Once you know how to make a budget it is important to do it every month. In fact it may take two to three months before your budgeting skills really begin to click. Just be patient with the process, because in the end it will help improve your overall financial situation.

What A Budget Does

As a personal financial planning tool, a written, monthly budget allows you to plan for how you'll spend and/or save your money each month and also keep track of your spending patterns. Though making a budget may not sound like the most exciting activity (and for some, it's downright scary), it's vital to keeping your financial house in order as budgets rely on balance. If you spend less in one area, you can spend more in another or choose to save that money for a larger future purchase, building a "rainy day" fund, or even for retirement.

Before you begin to make your budget, it's important to realize that in order to be successful you have to provide as much detailed and accurate information as possible. Ultimately, the end result of your new budget will show you where your money is coming from, how much is there, and where it's all going each month.

CHAPTER TWO
MONEY MANAGEMENT

Core Principals

Spend Less Than You Have Coming In By learning how to save, you naturally discipline your financial impulses. By unrestrained spending, people run up credit card debt, which can be extremely difficult to manage. By learning how to spend less than you have coming in allows you to save money for that rainy day that inevitably comes. When our financial sun is shining we tend to think it will be that way forever, don't we? But unforeseen events often can unexpectedly knock us off of our feet.

Losing one's job, an unplanned for baby, an accident, a health challenge, or a natural disaster can very quickly drain what little savings we have if any. By learning how to spend less than we have coming in and then carefully safeguarding that income can allow us to plan for a comfortable retirement or to use those funds when that rainy day comes.

One of the unexpected byproducts of this principle is that you have money to buy the nicer things in life. By following this strategy has allowed me to afford some of the things I want in life. It can for you too.

Learn To Distinguish Between Needs and wants. Many of us who have lived in abundance all of our lives grow accustomed to modern-day living. Modern-day transportation, plentiful food, good housing, sanitation, clean water and modern-day technical conveniences, opportunities for good education -- all have taken these things for granted. And consequently, the line between needs and wants gets conveniently blurred. We began to think we need that new car, that new washing machine, that new TV, but do we? Actually no. That's not to say modern-day conveniences are bad, they're clearly not. It is our attitude toward them that is at issue here, not the conveniences we enjoy.

Here's the point: When someone lives beyond their means, a host of problems inevitably ensue. The use of debt in living beyond our means allows us to prolong the day of reckoning but debt is a keen observer of dates and times and that day of reckoning will come.

It is an interesting financial phenomenon that one's needs expand when financial prosperity has already been attained. Such an attitude is due to pride, the inevitable byproduct of wealth or prosperity and that attitude is usually at the use of consumer debt itself in our society, and that leads to the next point...

Use Debt As a Financial Instrument of Necessity, Not As a Prime Financial Tool -- Use Credit Cards in Place of Cash for Safety Reasons

"Debt is a tanglesome net."

In a literal way, debt is bondage with your creditor having authority or command on you. It was said that "debt is a four-letter word." While this point was made in humor, it has some common-sense applicability.

Buying a home and paying for an education are the two main reasons to use debt. To use it for consumer purchases however, that is when one gets into dangerous territory. The instant gratification nature of consumer credit is a narcotic to many almost akin to the high the gambler addict feels and if not controlled could lead to financial ruin.

A good rule of thumb to use when considering going into debt for a consumer item is to ask yourself the question, "Do I really need this?" Needs involve the bare necessities like food, water, housing, and health. If it doesn't meet that criteria, then it is not a need. Replacing an old washing machine with a new one is an example of that. Can you perhaps have the old washing machine repaired instead of buying a new one? Can you make that old suit last a little longer instead of buying a new one? In most instances, the answer is almost always yes.

Last point for this subtopic -- use credit cards as cash either to avoid carrying a lot of cash around, which could endanger your personal safety, or just as a convenience. I use my credit cards all the time.

I use them to avoid carrying cash around yes, and I admit I use it to accumulate cash reward points, but I mainly use it for convenience.

And, here's the kicker: I always pay its balance in full when the bill comes due. Its only been a couple of times in my life that I've ever carried a credit card balance and that was only for one month as I inadvertently read the statement and paid only the minimum amount. I use the card the same as cash and always pay it off at statement time. The result? The credit agencies love me and I have a good credit score.

How To Save Money

It's important to learn how to save money, otherwise you will never improve your situation. You may already have high debt on your house and just want to start paying that off; the ideas in this book will help you do that as well.

This part of the book is mainly for people that have no assets or savings and need to start at the beginning. It's important to have these basic skills. Without it, you won't learn how to manage money. So even if your given a large sum of money, you wouldn't know how to handle it.

So this is for the people that wants to purchase a house and have no savings to do so. This will teach you how to save. The easiest way is to save 10% (or more) of your income.

So the best way to have the 10% saved, is to have your employer put 10% of your wage into another bank account, perhaps a bank that is not in your town or city and don't have a keycard or internet access to it. So the 10% just goes into their every week and you don't even know it.

Then you can spend the rest. This is a obviously slow process in order to get wealthy. For example, if your income is $50,000, then it's just $5000 per year going into it. But it's better than nothing.

So that's the BEST way of doing it. You know why? Because you don't see it so you can't spend it.

If you wait until your pay goes into your bank account and then transfer it yourself or have a direct debit set up, it's not the same. Then you need to work out how much you need to save if you have a goal, which you should have, since you read the chapter on goal setting.

If you have a goal to buy a $300,000 house in a years time then you will need the deposit and any closing costs. Lets say you need $40,000, so break that down to weekly. Assuming your income is $50,000, 10% of that is $5,000, so you need to get an extra $35,000.It may sound silly, once you get a goal, and start looking at ways to find money, you will find that you have other ideas that may pop up and other means will come your way.

When this happens you need to notice them. There is a name for this but we will call it 'luck' and when things start falling into place, and then take up all the opportunities that comes your way.

If your goal was a house in 1 years time - now you are on your way to buying your first house. If you have a house already then you are now paying it off quicker. Why do you want to pay your home your home loan off quicker?

The reason you want to do this is that you can use the equity - that is the difference from what you owe and how much it is worth, to buy another house - to rent out - or future investments. Wealth isn't built by owing lots of money, you need to start paying it off. Then you start building the equity.

The reason that you want to buy another house is that in the long term it will give you asset growth and an income in the form of rent.

Managing Money

1. *Don't Buy It Just Because It Is On Sale.*
When you are trying to get out of debt and to save money, this ends up being a waste of money. We purchase things not on our list, for the future or for someone else. If you want to get out of debt, you need to restrict your spending. The best way to get out of debt is to stop spending. You have to spend on your needs only, not wants. So, unless that item on sale is on your "NEEDS" list, do not purchase it.

2. *Write Down Your Expenditures.*
By writing down what you spend, even five cents, it becomes very obvious where your money is going and where you need to rein in. You may have heard of the expression "Don't nickel and dime yourself to death." So even if the item is inexpensive, it all adds up. Nickels turn into dollars. For example, let's say you treat yourself to a special coffee only once a week at $4.25. In a year that's about $221. So, when you are trying to get out of debt, don't think of that coffee as ONLY $4.25.... think of it as $221 in your Savings account! Think of it as two weeks of

groceries! Think of it as the interest you could have paid on your debt. I'm not saying you are not entitled to a treat once in a while, but when you want to get out of debt, then you have to forego some pain for the greater good. The time for treats will be when you reach your goals. You need to deprive yourself until you reach them, otherwise, nothing changes.

3. *Come Up With A Plan For Your Weaknesses.*
So if a special coffee is your weakness, then purchase the ingredients and learn how to make yourself a special coffee at home. I used my Air Miles to get an Espresso Machine, so it didn't cost me any money, and whenever we were in the mood for a special coffee, we go home and make one.

They are just as good and now I don't feel deprived. If you love having a manicure, why not learn how to give yourself one. It isn't the same, I know, but until you are debt free, you have to cut out the luxuries.

So, you may miss the relaxation of someone else doing it for you, but it will be so much better when you can go get a pedicure or manicure and PAY for it out of your Savings and not out of debt. Until then, you will have to go without, or give yourself one.

4. *Sleep On It Before Purchasing.*
I used to be an Impulsive shopper. I could reason my way into purchasing anything I wanted. But once I got out of the store, and away from the item, it helped me to remember and think objectively whether I "really" needed it. Sometimes I have concluded Yes, and gone back to find it sold. But 99% of the time I never went back. Most of the time we "think" we need it, but that is our heart talking. If you sleep on it, you are more objective. You may even realize that was not such a great deal after all.

5. *Look At Ways To Lower Your Monthly Expenses.*

We do not eat out at restaurants, we do not go to the theatre, we do not travel to vacation spots, all ways to reduce our expenditures. But then I realized we were spending too much money on our Security. With a phone call, we changed our package and are saving another $25 each month, and we don't even notice the difference. Another call to our cell phone company to find out how we can reduce our bill there. It never hurts to give them a call. Many times they will offer some suggestions because they do not want to lose you as a customer.

6. *Start Putting Money Into Savings.*

Even if you can't put very much. This is a good habit for a couple of reasons. It gets you into the habit of setting money aside, plus it starts building a cushion. If a bill comes you totally forgot about, then you won't be adding to your debt, you will have a cushion to handle it. So even if it is only $25 a month, start putting something into your Savings Account.

7. *Concentrate On Paying Off The Debt That Carries The Highest Interest.*

Even though I only have my mortgage to pay off, this is what I would do if I had Credit Card debt. The interest is killing you, so you need to kill it first and as soon as possible. Talk with your bank if you can compile your debt and get a lower interest as another option.

8. *Plan A Budget.*

I have tried over and over again, and this is one area took years to understand. Some people may write one out, others divide their money into envelopes. The reason for planning a budget is to put down what your actual income is on one side, and then your expenditures on the other. As long as you stick with it, then you can refrain from exceeding your income and get out of debt. I just deal with this by spending less, spending wisely, and spending only on your needs.

9. *No More Window Shopping....*
If you are on a diet, would you entice
yourself by going into a Bakery? That would
not be wise. So no more recreational
shopping. Your wants begin with your eyes,
so put your "eyes" on a diet. If you don't see
it, then you won't know it is out there, then
you won't want it. My weakness is once I
want something, it never leaves my mind
until I get it. I really want an iPad, and
someday I will have one, but not until I can
add it to my budget. So until then, I delete
the emails that Apple sends me.
Unsubscribe to those shopping websites.
Whatever it takes. It will be worth it in the
end. Until then, why tempt yourself.

10. *Keep Your Dreams & Goals Before You.*
Keep a constant reminder with you to help
keep you on track. Otherwise you will just
feel deprived and then falter to make
yourself feel better. But if you remember the
greater good, your reason "Why," it will give
you the will power you need to stay on track,
and you will be content with less until you
get there. You could post a picture of your
dream house, or have some beach scene as

your computer screen saver, whatever it is that is your goal. Then the deprivation now is SO worth it.

HOW TO SET UP A BUDGET AND STICK TO IT

Saving money at the grocery store is an awesome way to free up extra cash to spend in other areas or to just make ends meet. As we have seen, cutting your costs on groceries is definitely doable. If we work hard enough at it, we can really save a bundle. However, freeing up lots of extra cash and having the money just disappear elsewhere is not the best way to manage it. And, that brings me to my next biggest passion. Budgets. I am now a firm believer that we all need a budget. If we make $20,000 a year or if we make $500,000 a year. It does not matter. We all need to start a budget and stick to it.

So, here are some ways to help you manage your money and plan a budget for your family.

1. *Go through your income and expenses.*
Look at every single bit of income that comes in and every single bit that goes out. Write it all down. Everything. Every gift, every fast food purchase, everything. Once you have it all written down, start with the items that are due every month and can not be changed (at least not right away). Then make a list of the bills that you can adjust. So you should wind up with 2 outgoing expense categories: Fixed Bills and Variable Bills.

Fixed Bills: mortgage/rent, car payments, phone bills, etc.

Variable Bills: groceries, gas, dining out, entertainment, clothes etc.

2. *Write your budget: Get to work setting up your budget.*
If your mortgage/rent is $2000 and you are budgeting every 2 weeks, then $1000 per paycheck gets put aside for that. Go down the list and account for everything. If you

don't have enough then you will need to make adjustments. That is a must. Your outgoing cash MUST NOT exceed your incoming cash. If it does, then go to your variable bills and start cutting. If you have extra money leftover, then that should be used to either pay down debt, add to your emergency fund, savings account and/or retirement account.

3. *Emergency Fund*:
If you do not have an emergency fund, you need to add that to your budget line. Get yourself $1000 saved up as quickly as possible. If it means selling off some stuff on eBay/craigslist or at a garage sale then do it. If it means, eating out of your stockpile for a month or 2, then do it. It's very important to at least have a small emergency fund so when something goes wrong, you don't have to pull out a charge card to pay for it.

4. *Sticking with it.*

The key is to stick with it. It's easy to pull from one of your budgeted accounts one month to pay for another budget that has run dry. The typical thing to do is to say I'll pay it back next paycheck. Well, trust me when I tell you, 9 times out of 10 that won't happen. The money never gets back to where it should be and before you know it, a little hole has been dug that you are having trouble climbing out of. What happens next? Those credit cards come out to pay, not for fun stuff, but for the stuff you had on your budget that you can no longer keep up with.

So, STICK WITH THE BUDGET.

CHAPTER THREE
PLANNING THE BUDGET

In the previous chapters, we identified all costs and all income and now have a clear picture of the current situation. Using this information, the budget we set will, in effect, be an overview of how we live our lives from this point on. There will be certain rules that we have to stick with, but we will know that sticking to the rules will allow us to achieve our future financial goals.

The next part of the process is a little more painful and certainly more laborious than the last, but nevertheless must be done. Begin with the easy stuff first. This is the middle section on the budget sheet, i.e.:

- car expenses;
- food and housekeeping;
- miscellaneous goods and services;
- personal and leisure;
- sundries and emergencies.

There will be a lot of low hanging fruit here (easy savings to be made).

For example, let's say your daily expenditure diary reveals that on your commute to work you buy a newspaper at the railway station and a coffee while you wait for the train. You buy lunch at the deli around the corner, but go to the local pub for a sit down lunch and a drink on a Friday. You have a drink with colleagues after work on average 2 nights a week and buy an evening paper to read on the train on the way back from work. This is what this expenditure looks like over the week:

Morning coffee: 1.50 x 5 = 7.50
Morning paper: 0.60 x 5 = 3.00
Lunch at the deli 2.50 x 4 = 10.00
Bar lunch: 7.50 x 1 = 7.50
After work drinks: 2.80 x 2 = 5.60
Evening paper: 0.50 x 5 = 2.50
Weekly total: 7.50 + 3 + 10 + 7.50 + 5.60 + 2.50 = 36.10

Look at this again. Every single item is discretionary, yet it will cost you 144.40 in a 4 week month.

You may not be able to give everything up on the list, but taking a flask of coffee to work with a packed lunch may be a start. Many newspapers now offer yearly subscriptions that will cut the weekly bill by more than half - if you still need to have an actual newspaper every morning and every evening (do you?). The pub lunch could be dropped and the drinks with the colleagues after work cut back to one drink one evening a week - still sociable enough for most people.

In this example we might get back something like 130 per month. If there are two of you doing it, it might be more like 260 per month.

You need to do this type of breakdown and cost reduction exercise on each line item. Drop things like takeaways to a once a month treat and (if you do not already) learn to cook and cut out ready meals and other prepared food. You will not only save money, you will find you start living healthier too.

Examine closely how you do your motoring. Could you manage with one car instead of two? Could you get rid of the gas guzzling 4 x 4, which would reduce insurance, maintenance, road tax and fuel bills - all at once? Hopefully you are getting the idea by now.

Once the individual figures have been reviewed and cost reductions identified, you can put the new figures into the budget sheet and we can now start to see the new budget taking shape.

Next we can look at the first section. That is:
-housing costs;
-rates and utilities;
-important household services;
-personal insurances.

These are largely fixed costs, but there are opportunities here too. Housing costs such as rent or mortgages can be reduced.

Mortgage deals can be switched to take advantage of new lender deals, or fixed rate schemes taken on if interest rates look like rising in the near future. The term of the loan can be extended or (if things are really tight) payments dropped to interest only for a while. You need to ask the question.
If you are renting, could you manage with a smaller property, or a one in a less fashionable area? Could you move closer to work at the same time and reduce daily traveling costs?

Take a look at what seems to be fixed costs such as personal, or household, insurances and compare rates and benefits. Deals in this area change literally every week.

Gas and electric costs can be reduced by switching supplier or, better still, turning down the heating and switching off lights and appliances when they are not being used. Focus on this for a while and you might be pleasantly surprised at the difference it will make.

And so on.

The last cost section is the credit card and unsecured debt one. Much like insurances this may be a more flexible area than you think. If your credit rating is good then you have lots of room here to take on new cards and deals with 0% interest rates. Make sure when you do this that you close down the accounts you are transferring from. That is, you do not increase your overall indebtedness, or availability of debt.
If your credit rating is already poor, or bad, this may not be an option for you, so you will have to find other ways to reduce your repayments. One thing that creditors like to see is that their debtors are in control of the situation. A well put together budget sheet like the one we are in the process of outlining here can be a huge help.

Using the budget sheet you can identify all income and expenditure that needs to be made before handling your unsecured debt. This will leave you a set amount that can be used to negotiate reduced payments to your creditors.

This is a separate subject in its own right, but showing you are in control of your own finances may allow you to negotiate a reduced payment plan with the companies concerned.

Any other thing you can do in this area to consolidate debt and reduce overall interest payments needs to be examined closely.

However, you need to resist the temptation to make any loan consolidations that involve using your property for security. There is probably another way, so explore the other ways first.

The last section is income. You may have been tough with yourself in the cost section, but the other dimension to the budget is of course income. The more you increase your income, the less you need to cut back (or the bigger the benefit if you do).

In other words increasing income is not always about getting further up the greasy pole, sometimes it is about taking a sideways move into any area you had not considered before.

One last point on income: while you have the budget sheet in front of you it is worth evaluating the cost of work. In other words, when you add up travel, parking, fuel, dry cleaning, child care, work wear etc, then subtract it from your income. That will give you a true figure of what you earn.

Finalizing The Budget

The above represents a substantial investment in time and effort. The end result will be a budget sheet which is accurate, personally optimised and which puts you in control of your own finances.

Having made this effort, you should now have identified specific allowances for each item and you now need to be sure that money is allocated each month to cover those items whether they occur weekly, monthly, quarterly or yearly.

It is unlikely that you will be able to reduce all of your costs, move house, change jobs, etc, all at once, so you may have recognized already that this budgeting exercise can be a progressive thing that happens over time.

Therefore, to begin with, you will need to ensure that costs are under control and, as a minimum, outgoings equal income. Over time you will look for cost savings and income increasing opportunities and, once taken advantage of, you can then revisit the budget sheet, put in the new figures and move on.

One completely free benefit to all of this is that, once it is all complete and you are sticking to it, you get a full night's sleep whenever you want.

CREATING A BUDGET

Even if you don't use a budget spreadsheet, you probably need some way of determining where your money is going each month. Creating a budget with a template can help you feel more in control of your finances and let you save money for your goals. The trick is to figure out a way to track your finances that works for you.

The following steps can help you create a budget.

Step 1: Note Your Net Income

The first step in creating a budget is to identify the amount of money you have coming in. Keep in mind, however, that it's easy to overestimate what you can afford if you think of your total salary as what you have to spend. Remember to subtract your deductions, such as for Social Security, taxes, 401(k) and flexible spending account allocations, when creating a budget worksheet. Your final take-home pay is called net income, and that is the number you should use when creating a budget.

If you work freelance or part-time, we've put together some tips for managing irregular income.

Tip: If you have a hobby or a talent, you may be able to find a way to supplement your income. Having an extra source of income can also be helpful if you ever lose your job.

Step 2: Track Your Spending
It's helpful to keep track of and categorize your spending so you know where you can make adjustments. Doing so will help you identify what you are spending the most money on and where it might be easiest to cut back.

Begin by listing all your fixed expenses. These are regular monthly bills such as rent or mortgage, utilities or car payments. It's unlikely you'll be able to cut back on these, but knowing how much of your monthly income they take up can be helpful.
Next list all your variable expenses—those that may change from month to month such as groceries, gas and entertainment. This is an area where you might find opportunities to cut back. Credit card and bank statements are a good place to start since they often itemize or categorize your monthly expenditures.

Tip: Record your daily spending with anything that's handy—a pen and paper, an app or your smartphone. You can use this spending and budgeting tool if you have an account with Bank of America.

Step 3: Set Your Goals
Before you start sifting through the information you've tracked, make a list of all the financial goals you want to accomplish in the short-and long-term. Short-term goals should take no longer than a year to achieve. Long-term goals, such as saving for retirement or your child's education, may take years to reach. Remember, your goals don't have to be set in stone, but identifying your priorities before you start planning a budget will help. For example, it may be easier to cut spending if you know your short-term goal is to reduce credit card debt.

Step 4: Make A Plan
Use the variable and fixed expenses you compiled to help you get a sense of what you'll spend in the coming months. With your fixed expenses, you can predict fairly accurately how much you'll have to budget for. Use your past spending habits as a guide when trying to predict your variable expenses.

You might choose to break down your expenses even further, between things you need to have and things you want to have. For instance, if you drive to work every day, gasoline probably counts as a need. A monthly music subscription, however, may count as a want. This difference becomes important when it's time to make adjustments.

Step 5: Adjust your habits if necessary
Once you've done all this, you have what you need to complete your budget. Having documented your income and spending, you can start to see where you have money left over or where you can cut back so that you have money to put toward your goals.

Want-to-have expenses are the first area to look for spending cuts. Can you skip movie night in favor of a movie at home? Try adjusting the numbers you've tracked to see how much money that frees up. If you've already adjusted your spending on wants, evaluate your spending on needs. You may need internet at home, but do you need the fastest available?

Lastly, if the numbers still aren't adding up, you can look at adjusting your fixed expenses. Doing so will be much more difficult and require greater discipline, but on close inspection a "need" may just be a "hard to part with." Such decisions come with big trade-offs, so make sure you carefully weigh your options.

Tip: Small savings can add up to a lot of money, so don't overlook the little stuff. You might be surprised at how much extra money you accumulate by making one minor adjustment at a time.

Step 6: Keep checking in

It's important that you review your budget on a regular basis to be sure you are staying on track. You can also compare your monthly expenses to those of people similar to you. Few elements of your budget are set in stone: You may get a raise, your expenses may increase or you may have reached your goal and want to plan for a new one. Whatever the reason, keep checking in with your budget following the steps above.

HOW MONTHLY BUDGET THAT WORKS

You don't have to reach the end of the month wondering where your money went. Doing a budget is simply telling your money where to go. And if you're not good at budgeting yet, that's okay! It takes a little time. By your third budget, you'll be a pro.

- Write down your total income for the month.
- This is your total take-home (after tax) pay for both you and, if you're married, your spouse. Don't forget to include everything—full-time jobs, second jobs, freelance pay, Social Security checks,

and any other ongoing sources of income.

- List all your expenses.
- Think about your regular bills (mortgage, electricity, etc.) and your irregular bills (quarterly payments like insurance or HOA) that are due for the upcoming month. After that, total your other costs, like food, gas, and entertainment. Every dollar you spend should be accounted for.
- Subtract expenses from income to equal zero.
- This is called a zero-based budget, meaning your income minus your expenses should equal zero. If you're over or under, check your math or simply return to the previous step and try again.
- Track your expenses throughout the month.
- Once you start the budget, you'll still need to stay on top of your expenses. The good news is that EveryDollar makes tracking your expenses (and budgeting for them) extremely easy.

PERSONAL BUDGET

If you're hoping to gain more control over spending and begin working towards your financial goals, you need a budget.

A personal or household budget is an itemized summary of expected income and expenses for a defined period of time, typically one month. While the word budget is often associated with restricted spending, a budget should really mean more efficient spending.

A budget will show you how much money you expect to bring in against all of your expenditures from the required expenses like house payments and rent to discretionary spending like entertainment. Instead of viewing a budget as a negative, you can view it as a tool for achieving your financial goals.

How To Make Your Personal Budget

1. *Gather every financial statement you can.* This includes bank statements, investment accounts, recent utility bills, and any information regarding a source of income or expense. One of the keys in the budget-making process is to create a monthly

average, so the more information you can dig up the better.

2. *Record all of your sources of income.*
If you are self-employed or have any outside sources of income, be sure to record these as well. If your income is in the form of a regular paycheck where taxes are automatically deducted, then using the net income (or take-home pay) amount is fine. Record this total income as a monthly amount.

3. *Create a list of monthly expenses.*
Write down a list of all the expected expenses you plan on incurring over the course of a month. This includes a mortgage payment, car payments, auto insurance, groceries, utilities, entertainment, dry cleaning, student loans, retirement or college savings — essentially everything you spend money on.

4.*Break expenses into two categories: fixed and variable.*

Fixed Expenses are those that stay relatively the same each month and are required parts of your way of living. They included expenses such as your mortgage or rent, car payments, cable and/or internet service, trash pickup, credit card payments and so on. These expenses, for the most part, are essential yet not likely to change in the budget.

Variable Expenses are the type that will change from month to month and include items such as groceries, gasoline, entertainment, eating out, and gifts, to name a few. This category will be important when making adjustments.

5. *Total your monthly income and monthly expenses.*

If your end result shows more income than expenses, you are off to a good start. This means you can prioritize this excess to areas of your budget such as retirement savings or paying more on credit card balances to eliminate that debt faster. If you are showing a higher expense column than income, it means some changes will have to be made.

6. *Make adjustments to expenses.*
If you have accurately identified and listed all of your expenses, the ultimate goal would be to have your income and expense columns to be equal. This means all of your income is accounted for and budgeted for a specific expense or savings goal.

If you're in a situation where expenses are higher than income, you should look at your variable expenses to find areas to cut. Since these expenses are typically non-essential, it should be easy to shave a few dollars in a few areas to bring you closer to your income.

Budget Plan For Your Business
Planning For Success In Your Business
Do you feel like running from the room screaming when someone says, "Where's your budget?" Or what about "How much did you budget for that?"

Most people hate the idea of a budget. These are the people who have never had one. They feel that a budget is too confining and that it's something to avoid. Well, if that's you and you want to succeed in business - get over it! A budget actually puts you in control of the money you work so hard for and of your financial future.

First, adjust your thinking. Instead of seeing a budget as a restriction as to what you can do, see it as a tool for helping you plan to do as much or even more than you thought possible before. It's important to remember that a monthly budget isn't a hard and fast system that you have to follow rigidly. Many people avoid creating a budget because they feel it is too restrictive. The truth is that a budget is liberating. It's a plan that grows and adapts with you as your needs change.

When it comes to business, your monthly business budget forms the foundation of all of your business finances. Keeping a monthly budget make it easier to plan; stay out of debt; contract with the right people and services; make solid business decisions; and best of all, get and stay profitable.

There are a few simple steps to create your monthly budget plan.

Step 1: Choose The Planning Tool Right For You

Do you prefer to simply sit down with pen and paper? Check your local office supply store for simple accounting notebooks. Prefer using a computer? Use a word processing or spreadsheet application. I always prefer Excel when it comes to numbers as it is much easier to automate calculations in Excel than in Word tables.

Think you'd prefer to use a small business accounting program, but don't have the cash to invest at the moment? Do a quick Google search for "best free small business accounting software" to find one. Most programs have a budgeting feature.

Step 2: Determine Your Income Sources

Income is generally the first category for any accounting system. Think outside the box for a moment and think of all the ways you can make money. For instance, if you are working in information marketing you might have sales, commissions, affiliate marketing, etc. If you are still uncertain of all the ways you make money, take a look at the monthly statement from your bank or payment processor (such as PayPal). Look at where your money comes from and categorize it.

Put your income sources in a table of some kind. Make it five columns wide. The first column contains your income sources. Column 2 is what you actually made; name it "Actual." Title column 3, "Budgeted." In this column put in how much you thought you'd make that month. The budgeted column is what you use when determining your expense budget. More on that later...

Your fourth and fifth column are "Over Budget" and "Under Budget." As you might guess Over Budget is how much you earn over what you budgeted and budgeted to earn and Under Budget is for how much under your budged income you came. Obviously, you'll only fill in one of these two columns for each income category each month.

Step 3: List Your Monthly Expenses

Since some things you need to put into your monthly expenses come only once a year, you'll need to think in terms of all expenses. For example, you may only pay for your website hosting once a year, but you need to account for it some way. Take the total of any item you pay for only once a year and divide by 12 to come up with your monthly expense for that item.

Reviewing your bank statements can help you figure out your regular expenses. If you're just getting started in business and aren't sure, make some guesses. Remember, it's always better to overestimate your expenses than to underestimate them. Make another 5-column table. In the first column list your expenses by category and sub-category. For example, under the category Sales Expenses, you might have sub-categories of Affiliate Commissions, Advertising, and Shipping & Delivery. Under each category put the total for that category and save space for "Percent of Total." You'll figure out the percent of total later.

Now about that percent of total space...

This is useful planning data. Looking at these percentages you can easily see where you might be overspending by category. This helps you to know where to adjust your expenses when needed.

Just like with income the Actual, Budgeted, Over Budget, and Under Budget columns.

Step 4: Take Time For Your Monthly Summary

Once you have this all set up, set a time on your schedule at the end of each month to review all of the information to see how well you anticipated and planned. This information will help you create the next month's budget.

The basic formula you are working with is Income - Expenses = Profit. So, at the end of the month put a line at the top or bottom of your summary have another table that shows those figures along with the columns for actual, budgeted, over budget and under budget. Now a quick glance tells you how you did that month.

Step 4: Put Your Monthly Budgeting Plan into Action

Like with any plan, it is only good if you use it. To put your Monthly Budget Plan to use you'll need to create a system to keep your income and expenses organized. Decide whether you are going to add up your income and expenses daily or weekly and then stick with that plan. Whether daily or weekly, enter it as an appointment with yourself in your calendar.

You'll need to keep track of all invoices and receipts. Here's one way to do it. Staple the day's or week's expense receipts to one piece of paper with the total written. Take a second sheet of paper and do the same with the invoices. That way, when you sit down at the end of the month to review your budget and plan for the next month, you'll have all of the information readily available.

The first few months you may be off by quite a bit. However, as you learn to predict and anticipate income and expenses your budget will gain accuracy. Once you see just where your money is coming from and where it is going over time, you can make adjustments to it to meet your business needs.

CHAPTER FOUR
BUDGET PLANNING AND YOUR
FINANCIAL FREEDOM

Budgeting and Cash Flow.....two simple phrases that you would expect to learn the meaning of in grade school. If not, certainly by High School. Well guesswhat... NEITHER!!! I suspect this is the main reason why so many young people get into financial trouble at such an early age. They have no idea how the whole process works. Did you hear the joke about the newlyweds arguing...one says "Why do we always run out of money before the end of the month", the other one snaps back and said "We can't be out of money, we have plenty of checks left!" The truth of the matter is that without proper budget planning, your financial freedom will be at risk!

When starting out to prepare a budget you must keep one underlying principle at the front of your mind. That is Honesty is the best policy. When you first start out, you have to do some estimating. Here is where you have to be truthful to yourself.

For instance, if you are trying to figure out how much you spend on food each day. Don't forget the daily stop to Racetrack on the way to work, or the afternoon coffee at Starbucks, etc. A well thought out Budget will keep you on track to meeting any and all the goals that you set for yourself. Additionally, just write down everything on paper that you are going to need when budget planning will help you uncover all the black holes that mysteriously consume your paycheck, month after month. Once you have your Budget in place, honesty has to kick in again. You have to honestly try to stick to your Budget or else you will fail. It does not happen automatically. There will be certain parts of Budget Planning that you can put on auto pilot. Doing so will help you in your quest to achieve financial freedom.

So where and how does someone begin to make a Budget. Since I did not learn it in school either, it was a rather fortuitous encounter that started me on the road to never bouncing a check or never getting a collection phone call. Many years ago, while applying for a loan, the bank had some loan documents prepared for me to fill out. One of them was a Personal Financial Statement (PFS). I filled it out then and I have been filling one out every year since. I think it is the greatest tool to learn how to budget. If you have never seen one, go to your local bank branch and ask for a PFS. If they ask why, just say you are preparing to apply for a loan. Anyway, I haven't gotten one from the bank in a long time as it is very easy to make your own PFS. In a nutshell, here is what you do. Get a blank piece of paper and draw a line down the middle. At the top of the left side, title it INCOME, and at the top of the right side, title it EXPENSES. Now here is where the fun starts. Back to the left side...write down all your sources of monthly income on an after tax basis. This is important because you cannot pay bills with before tax income, meaning your gross paycheck number is of no value for this exercise. Also keep in mind that if you get paid weekly, take the after tax number and multiply by 52 and divide by 12 to get your true monthly after tax number which is higher than just multiplying your weekly number by four thanks to that extra week that will sneak in once every quarter.

When finished, add up the left side to get your total monthly income from which you can work your magic. Now move over to the right side. Start by listing all your monthly expenses that are fixed, meaning they are the same every single month as in your home mortgage and your car payment and your utility bill if you have balanced billing, which by the way if you do not have balanced billing, you should consider it as it will help you stay on track. When you are finished listing all your fixed monthly expenses, start listing all your variable monthly expenses. Here is where some estimation may occur. Do your best to guess and do not leave anything out. Don't forget birthday gifts, entertainment, bowling night, newspapers and the daily Java stop if it fits. Last, put in a miscellaneous category, because you know you are going to need it. Add up the right side. Is the number greater than or less than the left side? If it is less than the left side, you are in fine shape for performing budget planning. If it is less than the left side, you have some work cut out for yourself if you want to succeed with financial freedom.

If the answer above was positive or in other words, you are spending less than you are bringing home, then Congratulations.. You are in good company and on the path to financial freedom. You probably have some good habits drilled into you from your upbringing or some other source of financial know how. Let me ask you one question. When you listed all your expenses on the right side, did you make an entry for your self? I suspect you are addressing this most vital aspect of your finances. One other question. You did include credit card debt right? Is this number growing, declining, or remaining the same? Again, if you are in this camp, I suspect all is well on this front.

If the answer above was negative, well then you just might be related to the couple we spoke about in the beginning that runs out of money every month before running out of month! What to do? In a word...DISCIPLINE! It takes discipline to put your finances in order. One of the reasons that your number is negative is because you were honest enough to write down ALL your expenses and that is a good thing. However, your day of reckoning has arrived. Now you have to start doing some inner reflection. You must ask yourself "Of all those things on the expense side...Do I really need all that stuff?" Is a 6 monthly magazine subscriptions really necessary? Is it so important to go out to eat once a week? How about once a month instead! If you made that one change alone, not only would your budget planning look better, but when you actually did go out, it would take on much more significance. Believe it or not, it will bring you more pleasure than the "weekly grind" of going out to eat. If you don't like the word discipline, than I will throw out another word at you...TWEAKING. Time to start tweaking the right side of the sheet. Take a long hard look at every single entry, line by line to determine where you are going to tweak. This is the only way to make the right side fall in line with your resources. Sure you can increase the left side, but that is easier said than done.

CHAPTER FIVE
WHY BUDGETS DON'T WORK

You know from personal experience that the title of this book is absolutely, 100% true. You may not want to believe it, but your experience tells you otherwise. Think about it. What is the purpose of a budget? To save money. But ask yourself this: Why would you need to save your money, if you are creating abundance in your life?

When you focus on prosperity, then that is your reality. When you focus on lack, then that is your reality. You cannot focus on both prosperity and lack at the same time. The same way you cannot be sad and happy at the same time, you cannot experience abundance and scarcity at the same time.

Have you ever stopped to ask yourself why you want to save money? Are you saving for a big purchase, or perhaps for an unexpected emergency? A "rainy day" mentality cannot coexist with a prosperity mentality. One cancels the other out.

So, if you choose to focus your efforts on saving a penny here, a dollar there, then you will. You absolutely will save a penny and a dollar. But what could you have done with the same amount of energy focused on creating wealth instead? Instead of focusing on saving money you already have, you could focus on making more money.

When your goal is to save, you always end up with less money than when you started. When your goal is to make money, you always end up with more money than when you started.

Why You Just Can't Stick to a Budget
Do you know why so many people can't seem to stick to a budget? It is because the mere fact that they are focusing on ways to spend less causes them to earn less. In order to do a budget, you first have to write down how much money you have coming in. Do you really want to tell the Universe that this number, whatever it is, is the amount of money you are willing to work with?

A budget assumes there is a finite amount of funds coming in, which in actuality, is lack thinking. It assumes there a set amount with which you must conduct your business, support your family, and indulge your whims every once in a while.

With a budget, you set spending caps for each expense category, based on the total amount of revenue you have coming in. You look at each expense carefully to see where you can cut, slash, and eliminate spending altogether. In fact, this is the opposite of what you should be doing if you want to grow your business and increase your personal wealth.

As stated above, lack thinking causes people to earn less. Not only is your energy focused on saving a dime, but the areas of your business that need the most capital are most likely not getting it. How much do you spend on targeted marketing? How much do you spend on increasing your knowledge of your market? How much do you spend on improving customer service? Again, when you focus on ways to spend less, you earn less.

When you earn less, you quickly blow your budget, because you no longer have the income you planned for. This is why it is impossible for most people to actually stick to a budget.

Going Broke on a Budget
Too many financial "gurus" preach budgeting. In fact, lessons in how to budget are a huge part of most financial information products. The countless Books and articles written about how to budget properly all keep you focused on being broke.

If you are constantly trying to stick to your budget, then you are constantly in a lack consciousness mindset. When you view your business as not having enough to pay expenses, so much so that you need to cut expenses, you are the captain of a ship that is sure to go down.

The negative effects of being "budget-minded" is more than a concept, it has a direct affect on your ability to keep your existing customers, and attract new ones. When you choose the cheapest, most economical way of doing business, you reduce the perceived value of your products or services.

Everyone wants to feel that they are getting a good value for their money. When you "cheap out" your customers will feel it. Very quickly you will lose customers, and eventually, you will lose your business.

Lack consciousness also creates a pervasive feeling of desperation, which can also be felt by your customers. Who wants to give their hard earned cash to a business that appears to desperately need money, and is cutting corners left and right?

When you give more value to your customers than they give in payment to you, your business will grow exponentially. Customers feel excited and special when they know they are getting a great deal for their money. A good way to keep your customers is to consistently provide them with more quality than they expect, and you can't do that if you are worried about saving a nickel.

Let's say you have four phone lines, and in your effort to stay on budget, you cut two of them. Now, in exchange for saving $60-$80 per month, you have frustrated customers who can't get through to you, and potential new customers who will move on to your competitors at the first sound of your recorded voice mail message.

No one, not even your customers, would begrudge you cutting unnecessary costs, or looking for a good value in your own vendors. But you can make those decisions on a per-cost basis. When it comes time to pay the bills, or commit to a new monthly expense, determine at that time if it will have a benefit to your customers or not.

Trade in Your Lack Mindset for a Prosperity Mindset
If by now you have not been convinced to abandon your budget, consider the fact that your lack thinking pinches off the flow of money to you, and to everyone else. We are

all connected. When you are in prosperity consciousness, you create more wealth for yourself, and for all of us. Think of it as doing your part for society.

How do you trade in your lack mindset for a prosperity mindset? Start by shifting your focus from saving to giving. The energy of giving to others, whether it is of your pocketbook, your time, or your heart, attracts more giving. Not only will you attract giving back to yourself, but your giving will also cause a chain reaction that attracts more giving to everyone.

Apply the act of giving to your business, and watch the money start to flood in. Give to your customers; don't shortchange them. Make sure you offer the best products on the market, the best customer service, and the best environment for them to conduct business with you.

Give your customers the best of you, by constantly improving your knowledge and expertise, so that they may benefit from it. If you read one book pertaining to your niche market per month, you will be one of the top experts in your field. That is how you create abundance and value for your customers. Focus your attention on how to give your customers the most value, and they will happily give you the price you set. You can only cut costs so much before there is nothing left, but your earning potential is limitless.

Of course it is true that some business owners lose track of their expenses, and may find themselves in a hole so big, they just can't dig their way out. A prosperity mindset does not mean that you disregard your expenses entirely. The goal here is not to avoid your bottom line, but to increase it. You can't do that if you blindly write checks and ignore your bank balance.

All successful business owners know how much is going out and what it's for - they just don't worry about how much it costs. Instead, they focus on how much value it will give their customers, and how much income it will generate. If an expense will not deliver value or the potential for increased revenue, by all means cut it.

CHAPTER SIX
BUDGET SUCCESS

You've analyzed your past expenses, put them into spreadsheets, loaded Quicken with all of your data and come up with a budget. Now what? The tough part! You actually have to stick to your budget and put your plans into action. This is easier said than done. In many cases you will have forgotten about your budget and your financial goals 6 months or a year down the road. How do you keep this from happening to you?

Here's how. Make sure you follow some of these tips below so this doesn't happen to you.

1. **Create a budget with realistic targets**

Let's say one of your budget goals is to not eat out for lunch or dinner on a regular basis. If you are honest with yourself you may find this to be an unrealistic goal. Sometimes it's a nice break to eat out and have a relaxing rewarding evening. In other words, don't set the bar too high.

Drastic and unrealistic goals are one of the surefire ways your budget will not succeed.

2. **Budget for expenses that don't occur on a routine basis**

Make sure you give consideration to expenses that occur once a year, such as holiday presents, birthdays, vacations, weddings, car maintenance costs, etc. These expenses don't occur every month and they will bust your budget plans wide open. Make a list of these events on a calendar and put a dollar figure to them. Place them in the month they are expected to occur so you can plan in advance how you will pay for them. The regular routine expenses are not the reason your budget will fail. It is these "gotchas" that will wreck havoc on your budget if you don't plan for them.

3. **Put your budget in writing**

Take the time to write down your budget plans. Making a mental note of your budget goals is a recipe for failure. Don't assume that your financial future will take care of itself by making a simple mental note to yourself. If you have your budget goals detailed in writing you can review and remind yourself weekly and monthly of your financial goals.

4. **If you have a bad month or week, don't give up!**

Let's say you have been reaching your budget goals for three months. In the fourth month, for whatever reason, you didn't reach your budget goals. Maybe you even stopped trying to stick to your budget! If this happens, don't just throw your hands up in the air and admit to failure. Everyone falls off the wagon sometimes. Your budget is a journey. There will be bumps in the road, so the key is to realize that everyone makes mistakes. This relates to a story that my mentor told me about an old time golfer. Before each round of golf, he told himself that he would have 4 or 5 bad shots. During the golf round, if he hit his ball into a bunker, he would tell himself, "There is one of my bad shots that I was expecting", hit the ball out of the bunker and move on. It didn't phase him one bit because he knew there would be some bad shots in his round.

5. **Adjust your budget over time** - This one is a biggie! It can take months or even years to fine tune a personal budget. When you initially made your budget plans, you probably had to guess at some of your figures. They might not have been in touch with the realities of every day life. For example, you may have underestimated your monthly grocery or utility bills. If this happens, analyze all of the underlying money that was spent in this category to see if your initial estimate was unrealistic. If it was, try to come up with a more accurate number and then stick to that new figure. It is this type of adjustment that is one of the keys to making sure you can stick to your budget.

6. **Review your budget every month**
This is where you will make any adjustments that are needed. Set aside the first day of each new month to review your income and expenditures and match them to your budget goals. By actively reviewing your finances and comparing it to your budget, you can adjust your spending habits. This gives you a chance to analyze areas that exceeded your budget expectations and

make the adjustments in your spending habits or your budget. The goal here is to not forget about your budget. One tip that has worked for me is to put a printout of my basic budget goals on the refrigerator. That way every day, several times a day, I would notice my budget goals sheet. I may not read it every time, but I notice it and it reminds me that I need to stick to my budget. That is why tip number 3 is so important.

7. **Set specific short-term goals**

Let's say one of your budget goals is to have all of your credit card bills paid off in two years. If your credit card balances total $20,000 that would be $10,000 a year. Divide that number further into quarterly reductions in your credit card bills, in this case $2,500 every 3 months. Now, this is a more tangible budget goal to shoot for isn't it? I find that when I divide intermediate and long term goals into short-term tangible stepping stones, I am able to feel a greater sense of accomplishment and am more likely to succeed.

8. **Reward yourself**

That's right! Treat yourself when you reach some of your short-term goals. Since your financial budget is really a journey, take some time to smell the roses on your way. Sticking to your budget should not be a restrictive, unpleasant experience. Not only should you take the time to enjoy your financial accomplishments along the way, but use part of your budget for fun things that you enjoy. Just make sure your rewards don't end up breaking your budget!

9. **Pay yourself first**

I'm sure that one of your budget goals is to save and invest a portion of your income. One of the keys to make sure you succeed at this is to do what the IRS does with your paycheck, take it out of your discretionary income immediately. This way, the money is saved away right off the bat. Move the money immediately into a savings or mutual fund account. Many mutual fund companies can setup automatic deductions from your paycheck. Despite your best intentions to save, the hectic, daily demands of life can reduce the amount you are able to save.

10. **Attitude is everything**

When most people think of a budget, they picture restrictions and pain. Almost like a diet. You know what happens with most diets? They don't seem work for long! First, if your budget is too strict, too restrictive on your spending, it won't work either. However, you will need to limit your spending in some areas and this will take some adjustment in your attitude. I found that when I am feeling limited and sorry for myself when I can't purchase something that I want, I remember my financial goals I set with my budget. I think about the satisfaction I feel when I reach those goals. Over time, you find that you don't want to disappoint yourself by breaking your spending goals on a spur of the moment purchase. Now, I actually get more pleasure knowing that I am reaching my budget goals when the thought of an impulse purchase crosses my mind.

Ways Budgeting Can Improve Your Life

These are cliches concerning money and most are true. Cliches are sayings that become cliche because there's a truth behind them.

"A fool and his money will soon part."

"A penny saved is a penny earned."

"Save for a rainy day."

All of these are true. But here's one that all people should choose as a mantra.

"Live within your means."

It means, quite simply, that you have to spend less than you take in. Creating a budget is easy. It's simple math. But for many people, creating and sticking to a budget are difficult at best.

There are several ways to do it. Some use a percentage basis, where each expense allows a certain percentage of income. Some even go so far as to put money in envelopes each month and pay from envelopes, but that's extreme, yet very effective.

Creating and sticking to a budget is an essential life skill they should teach in high school. It requires taking a hard look at your financial situation, being disciplined, and making it part of your everyday life. It should become ingrained.

Seven Reasons Why Budgeting Is Important
1. **It gives you a peace of mind**.
When you have the ability to quit living paycheck to paycheck, it is a great burden off your mind. You relax. You spend less time worrying about what's going on, which allows you to focus on work, family and enjoying life. When you have money worries, it is easy for other things to suffer.

2. **It helps you manage your debt or stay out of debt**.
As a rule, Americans carry too much personal debt. Sticking to a budget enables you to control spending, which means that if a need arises, you have the funds available or the skills to meet the need head on.

3. **It helps you save money**.

When you have a handle on your expenses, you get to save. In fact, saving should be the first thing you do when you establish your budget. Set aside somewhere between five and ten percent to save. Within your savings, you can create a mini-budget that includes:

Retirement

College Fund

Vacation

New Car

Second Home

4. **It helps you in emergencies**.

Car repairs, house repairs, an emergency room visit... all of these qualify as "emergencies." Paying for these things are often done on credit cards, which in turn adds strain to monthly payments. The emergency fund also covers job loss or temporary reduction in income, so the fund will be quite substantial... about three months worth of monthly expenditures.

Warning: Emergencies are things that will significantly alter your life or your ability to maintain necessary parts of your life. Medical, transportation, home... if something disastrous happens, you dip into the fund. Buying a new car is not an emergency; fixing one is if it means the difference between getting to work or not.

5. **It helps you control spending**.
Many people are in a situation where it is too easy to spend money. They don't actually have to have cash. It makes it easy to lose track of where the money is going and they get themselves into a bad situation.

If you know exactly how much is coming in, you know exactly how much is going out. If you add up all the small expenses, sometimes you find that those things you don't really need cost more than the things you do need. Prime example: Eating lunch out of the office averages $8 a day. A cup of coffee at a gourmet shop is about $3.50. If you bring lunch from home, not only is it better for you, but at roughly $2 per meal it saves $120 a month. A $10 can of coffee will last for a month, versus the $70 a month for habitual gourmet coffee shop patrons.

At the time of purchase, we don't think much about it. But those things add up over a month and can be quite surprising. Once you get into the habit of saving receipts and tracking all expenditures, it's easier to see how they add up.

6. **It helps you build a credit rating**

In the real world, people finance their houses and sometimes, their vehicles (but they shouldn't do... ever!) A good credit rating helps you save money on your mortgage and these days, potential employers are even pulling credit reports when considering you for a position. Yes, it happens when you sign the document that says they can do a background check.

A better credit rating means you could be charge 1/2 of one percent difference on your mortgage. On the average, on a $150,000 house, the difference between 5.5% and 6% is about $50 a month. Doesn't seem like much, does it? Works out to $600 a year. That sounds like "real money" now. Over the course of a mortgage, that's $18,000.

There are other savings, too, such as saving on mortgage insurance, and programs vary from lender to lender, but it paints a picture. So having a good credit rating saves you money by allowing banks to offer you better percentage rates because you're a good risk.

7. **It helps you teach kids about money**
Money management skills is an essential part of life, and the more your kids know about it, the more successful they will be. Only recently have schools been teaching these skills, but kids need to see it in practical use. If the knowledge is ingrained as part of their everyday life, they will be more likely to adhere to a budget.

CHAPTER SEVEN
GETTING YOUR BUDGET UNDER CONTROL

Most people have a lot of difficulty creating and sticking to a balanced budget. They might come up with one easily enough that looks good on paper, but putting it into practice is another story. If you're trying to get out of debt and build wealth but you're struggling with a budget that is out of control, I have some good news for you. You can get your budget under control, and I'm going to give you 5 keys for doing just that.

Know What's Coming In

Believe it or not, a lot of people can't tell you how much they make, let alone what their bring-home pay is. Obviously, a budget needs to be based on what you bring home, not on your gross salary. How you are paid also affects your income. Are you paid weekly? Every two weeks? Twice a month? Once a month? If you're a teacher you may only get paid 9 months out of the year and then have 3 months with no income. All of these scenarios will affect how you budget and whether or not the budget you create will work.

Really, I don't even like the word "budget." I prefer "spending plan." Most people think of a budget as something that tells them the maximum they can spend in any given category. Whatever is left over they can do what they want with. The problem with budgeting like that is you tend to blow through a lot of money that you'd be better off allocating for a specific purpose.

So, first figure out how much you have coming in. Then you're ready to move on to the second key.

Know Where Your Money is Going

Most people are surprised when they determine where their money is going at just how much of it goes to impulse spending - and I'm not just talking about those items that are strategically on display at the check stand. What about when you're surfing the net, doing research on eBay, or Craigslist, Amazon, or one of the other major internet retailers; are you able to just say no, or do you add items to your shopping cart impulsively... after all, it's only $25. There was a time when I would make one "small" purchase after another on the internet, only to discover I had somehow managed to spend $200!

When you determine where your money is going you need to then separate that into categories. What expenditures are necessities and which ones are extras? This is the first category you will want to rein in. Don't eliminate it; just make sure you set aside a realistic amount for some non-essential purchases. Otherwise, you will feel deprived and blow your financial diet completely.

Basically, you are going to start with giving, followed by savings, followed by necessities and then your non-essential purchases. If you have more left over at the end, you can either apply that amount to debt elimination, savings or giving.

Know Where You Want to Go
You have to have a plan. Spending is largely emotional. We overspend when we're feeling depressed or sorry for ourselves. We overspend when we are happy about a tax refund and feel we deserve a treat. We increase our living expenses when we get a

raise to equal the amount of the extra income - after all, we deserve that too Right!

What I'm suggesting is that you have an end goal in mind that is so emotionally driven that it will be painful for you to spend money outside of your spending plan.

If you truly want to retire and enjoy at least the same standard of living you have now, then it will be important for you to save money for your retirement. I can guarantee you that Social Security will not maintain your current lifestyle for you. No matter what your annual report says about how much you will get every month when you retire.

If you really want to go on that vacation to Africa, you will find it easy to do without your daily latte in the morning and energy drink in the afternoon. We don't have any trouble making sacrifices if we feel that the end result is worth it.

That's where most people fail when creating a budget. They have a vague feeling that they should budget, because someone told them it was a good idea. But, they don't own the idea. They haven't given it substance. It isn't real to them. So, the first time something comes along with an emotional impact, they whip out their wallet and write a check or, worse yet, put it on a credit card going into debt for something they don't need and probably won't even want anymore by the time it's paid for.

Develop a Little Flexibility
It will probably take you a few months before you really have a workable budget. It's easy to underestimate how much you will need for groceries. It's also easy to forget that the electricity bill may vary by a hundred dollars when the weather is very cold or very hot. It's easy to forget about those payments that aren't monthly, but still have to be paid quarterly, every six months, or annually. Then of course, there are unexpected emergencies, like your car breaking down on your way to work.

Leaving these things out of your budget can really mess you up. If you don't maintain an attitude of flexibility, you may be tempted to just quit. Just remember to remain flexible, change your budget here and there, and tweak it until you get it just right.

Have an Accountability Partner

It's definitely easier to stay on track if you have an accountability partner. If you're married, then your spouse should be your accountability partner. You'll want to sit down weekly in the beginning to see where you are and whether or not your spending plan is working. If you are single, see if one of your friends would like to team up with you and you can keep each other on track. Another option is to find a class or group focused on getting out of debt or budgeting (or both).

CHAPTER EIGHT
DEBT ELIMINATION

When it comes to debt we all have some, but some of us have more than others. There are ways to make sure you can eliminate your debts once and for all and more importantly that you stay out of debt for good. You need to know how to properly budget so that you can get rid of all your debts and move on with your life.

The biggest mistake people make when they budget is they do not save any money. You always have to save something because unexpected things happen and you need some money in reserve for these things. You do not want to find out that your car would not start today and it is going to cost you a few hundred dollars to fix that you just don't have.

When you are learning how to properly budget you also need to make sure you include all your bills and not just the ones that you pay on a weekly, daily, or monthly basis. You have other bills like your license tag renewal, oil changes, and other bills that are not paid monthly, but maybe quarterly or yearly. You need to estimate these and include them in your budget.

The last tip you need for how to properly budget is to make sure that you are including some money for yourself to have fun or do something you enjoy. Sure when you are paying off debts you have to cut way back, but you still need to find time to do something you enjoy like go out on a picnic, go to the movies, or something.

CHAPTER NINE
HOW TO MAKE A BUDGET WORK FOR YOU

If you feel like you are always broke, you have come to the right place. Having no money is never fun, we all know that, but many of us don't realize it doesn't have to be this way. Even without making more money, you can have more money. The idea is that you spend less.

What? Spend less money? We all know that we should probably spend less, we just don't realize how simple it really is. If you need to spend less money in order to have more money, you need to learn how to make a budget and how to make it work for you.

First, keep track of where you spend your money for at least 2 weeks. Write down every penny from your car insurance to the cup of coffee you buy before work everyday. Also write down all the money you make including all income sources. Subtract your expenses from your income.

Do you get a negative or positive number? If you get a positive number, that is very good. If you get a negative number, that is very bad. Zero means you break even. If you have a negative number, that means you are going into debt. Your goal should be to get a positive number.

Now is when you make a budget. Look at all your expenses and rate them. Which ones can you not live without and which ones do you not need? This is where you have the opportunity to make a budget work for you. Try to make it fit your lifestyle but be reasonable. The idea is to spend less money, so you will need to cut back somewhere.

By rating your items from high to low priority, you can make necessary changes. Some people will only need to make minor changes to make it work for them. Others will need to make very big changes. For example, If you're net worth, income minus expenses, is negative $1,000 or more, you need to make some big changes. You are living beyond your needs. If the cutting the small expenses isn't working, you'll need to think big.

Are you driving a car with huge monthly payments? Sell it and buy used. Are you living in a 3 bedroom apartment costing two grand a month or a house with a huge mortgage? You can either downgrade or rent out extra rooms.

By customizing your own budget, you can make it work and save lots of money in the process. Saving money over time can earn you even more by investing and help you feel more financially secure.

STEPS TO A BUDGET MADE EASY

Are economic troubles causing you to consider your personal financial situation? You may be worried about losing your job or how much debt you have. Avoid a potential personal financial crisis; get back to basics with a budget you can stick to. Here's how to start:

Step 1: **Set Realistic Goals**

Goals for your money will help you make smart spending choices. Ask yourself: What do I want my finances to look like in one year? Decide what's important to you and start there.

Step 2: **Identify your Income and Expenses**

You probably know how much you earn each month – but do you also know where it all goes? Find out by tracking what you're spending. Spend as you normally would, but for a few weeks, jot down every cent you spend. It's easy and you may be amazed by what you find out. More info on this

Step 3: **Separate Needs and Wants Ask yourself**: Do I want this or do I need it? Will spending this money get me closer to my financial goals or further away? Can I live without it? Set clear priorities for yourself and the decisions become easier to make. Learn more

Step 4: **Design Your Budget**
Make sure that you are not spending more than you make. Balance your budget to accommodate everything you need to pay for. One easy way to do this is with a easy-to-use budget calculator spreadsheet and worksheet that you can google and doenload online.

Step 5: **Put Your Plan into Action**
Match your spending to when you receive your income. Decide ahead of time what you'll use each pay check for. Ask yourself: Have I allocated money for my necessities (housing, food, utilities, transportation, etc.)? Have I put money aside for my debt payments, unexpected expenses, savings and the fun stuff? This will protect you from going into debt further because you won't rely on credit to pay for your living expenses.

Step 6: **Seasonal Expenses**
You know that things will "just come up" – school expenses, new shoes or an annual membership. Set money aside to pay for

these expenses so you can afford them without going into debt. More on this

Step 7: **Look Ahead**
Getting on track with a budget can take a month or two. You've lived all this time without a spending plan, so give yourself time to adjust.

CONCLUSION

Your Budget will work if your goal is to tap into the flow of abundance, expand your business, or create unlimited wealth. Budgets work if you have a vision for the life you want to manifest, or a dream you want to create. Budgets works for the best of the best, the millionaires, or the success stories - and they will work for you.

Last, make sure you follow your budget. Do not stray. Make sure there is enough of a padding in your budget that you can spend a little to reward yourself each week for following your budget. Maybe take the family out for dinner and a movie or go camping at the end of the month if you successfully follow your budget. This needs to be in your budget as well or you will have trouble with how to make a budget.